The AQS Guide
to Quilt Care

3rd Revision

by AQS Certified Quilt Appraisers
Bobbie A. Aug
Carol Butzke
Linda Honsberger
Gerald Roy

Located in Paducah, Kentucky, the American Quilter's Society (AQS) is dedicated to promoting the accomplishments of today's quilters. Through its publications and events, AQS strives to honor today's quiltmakers and their work and to inspire future creativity and innovation in quiltmaking.

© 2011, American Quilter's Society

Executive Book Editor: Andi Milam Reynolds
Graphic Design: Lynda Smith
Illustrations: Barry Buchanan
Cover Design: Elaine Wilson & Michael Buckingham
Photography: Charles R. Lynch unless otherwise noted

Additional copies of this book may be ordered from the American Quilter's Society, PO Box 3290, Paducah, KY 42002-3290, or online at www.AmericanQuilter.com.

Cover quilt courtesy of Helen Squire. Untitled, 80" x 83", documented 1872.

Acknowledgments

Thanks to Bobbie A. Aug, Carol Butzke, Linda Honsberger, and Gerald Roy for their assistance with this revised edition.

American Quilter's Society
P. O. Box 3290 • Paducah, KY 42002-3290
www.AmericanQuilter.com

Contents

Introduction

Years of experience appraising quilts have taught us the best ways to care for the quilts you love.

On the one hand, you want to use your quilts, whether as bed covers or wallhangings, but on the other hand, using them wears them out.

The information compiled in this booklet will help you protect the time, money, and emotion you have invested in making new quilts or collecting or inheriting old ones, and help you pass them on in the best possible condition to future generations.

DRESDEN PLATE, 1st quarter 20th century, Southern Appalachia. Courtesy of Andi Milam Reynolds. Damage occurred when the quilt was improperly washed in a washing machine in 2004.

Quilt Preservation, Conservation, and Restoration

To preserve or conserve a quilt is to stabilize it in its current condition; repair is sometimes called for. To restore a quilt is to return it to its original condition; repair is almost always required.

The quilt care discussed in this booklet aims to preserve or conserve, that is, to allow you to continue to use the quilt, which means continued wear. We recommend that you seek the advice of a qualified professional textile conservator or restorer if restoration is warranted, for example, if your quilt has historic significance or if you plan to retire it from use. See page 44 for ways to locate qualified professionals.

General Maintenance

Textiles are sensitive to light, chemicals, dust, dirt, oils, smoke, stains, perfumes, insects, pests and other animal (pet) activity, and unnecessary cleaning. Odors and moisture can also be absorbed to a quilt's detriment.

Minimal handling will avoid damage from body oils. Use clean white gloves or wash your hands frequently.

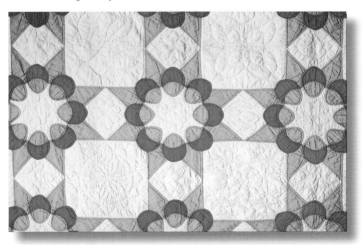

Quilt, detail. Full quilt on page 13.

Basic Quilt Care

Control the Light the Quilt Receives

Avoid direct sunlight; it fades textiles. Indirect sunlight will also fade quilts, so use care when placing wall quilts. Draw curtains in rooms where quilts are used on beds, or place a sheet over the quilt when drapes are open.

Fluorescent light, including compact fluorescent lights, should be filtered. See Resources on page 44 for a light filter source.

Incandescent light should be at least 10 to 12 feet away from quilts and used sparingly; it is a hot light.

Spotlighting quilts is not recommended; seek the advice of an independent lighting specialist if this is your aim.

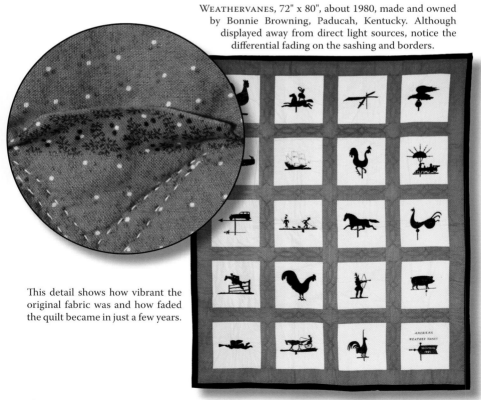

WEATHERVANES, 72" x 80", about 1980, made and owned by Bonnie Browning, Paducah, Kentucky. Although displayed away from direct light sources, notice the differential fading on the sashing and borders.

This detail shows how vibrant the original fabric was and how faded the quilt became in just a few years.

Provide a Stable Environment

Humidity at 50 percent and temperature at 60 to 70 degrees is recommended. Fluctuations stress the textile fibers, so storing quilts in an attic, unheated guest room, or other place where temperature and humidity are uncontrolled is unwise. Do not display or store quilts near heat vents.

Using Quilts

Many modern quilts are made to be slept under. We know from antique quilts used on beds that binding wears out more quickly than the rest of the quilt. To prolong the binding's life, first, make a double-fold binding, which will last longer than single-fold binding. Second, consider attaching a removable "chin guard" along the edge of the quilt nearest the head of the bed. This plain piece of muslin (or fabric that matches the border) can be tacked on, tied on, buttoned on, or attached with hook-and-loop tape for easy removal, because often what prompts the need to wash a quilt is the soiled edge around our heads/chins. Wash the chin guard instead and save both use and washing wear on the quilt.

Store Properly

Quilts should be aired or vacuumed before storing (see page 15 for proper vacuuming method). To air a quilt, place it on a flat clean surface (cover the surface with a sheet if necessary) and cover the quilt with a clean cloth or sheet. Do not air quilts in direct sunlight.

Ideal storage is a flat surface lined with acid-free material, large enough for each quilt or textile to have its own space. An alternative is to stack quilts flat on a bed, one on top of another, rotating them every three months so those on the bottom are not compressed.

Basic Quilt Care

When folding quilts, use crumpled acid-free tissue in the folds for support. For fabrics with plant origins such as cotton or linen, use *unbuffered* acid free tissue; for fabric with animal origins such as wool or silk, use *buffered* acid free tissue. Re-fold every three months to minimize permanent fold lines. Consider folding quilts on the bias so thread stress is minimized.

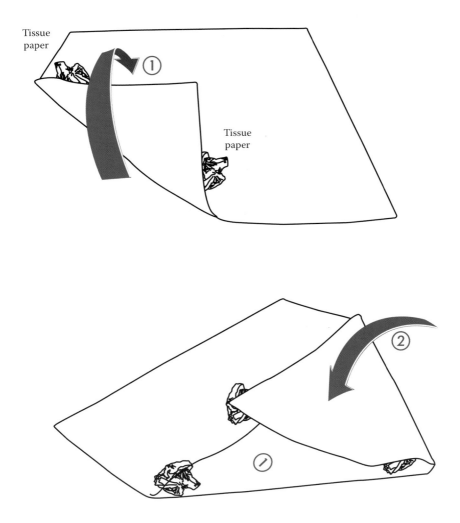

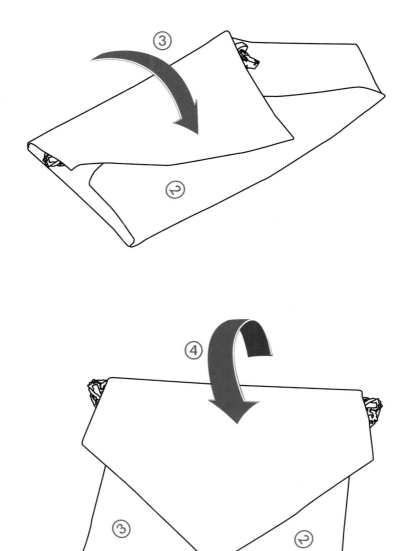

Basic Quilt Care

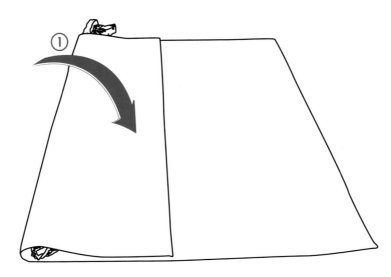

STEP 1- Tri-fold

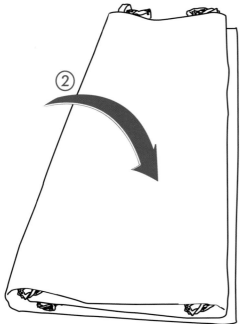

STEP 2- Tri-fold

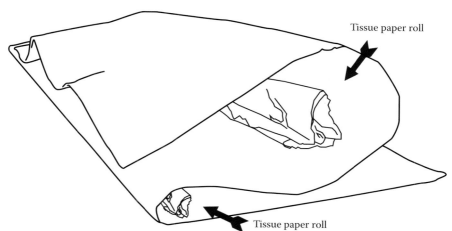

Tissue paper roll

Tissue paper roll

Z-fold/Accordion fold

Cover quilt, detail

Basic Quilt Care

Rolling quilts around a tube is a shipping or short-term storage option, but this procedure places stress on the entire quilt and is not recommended for the long term. When placing the quilt on the tube, roll so that the front side of the quilt is facing outward.

If the storage container is made of wood or cardboard, it should be lined with several layers of washed white cotton or unbleached muslin with no fragrances or softeners in the wash/rinse water. The liner should be washed every three months. Avoid using polyurethane plastics as shelf liners; these allow the off-gassing of wood acids. If using aluminum foil to line shelves, the heavy duty variety is easier to manage as it is less likely to tear.

Wherever quilts are stored, covers of prewashed and unused cotton sheeting, muslin, or pillow cases or acid-free tissue paper are strongly recommended. These materials allow air to pass through yet keep light and dust out. Plastic is not advised for storage unless you live in an arid climate.

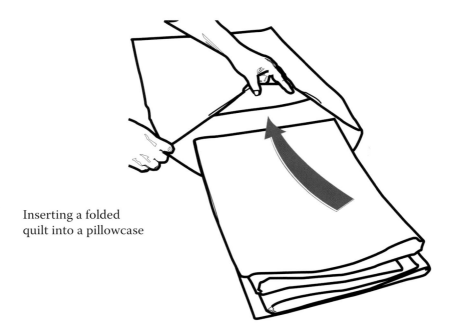

Inserting a folded
quilt into a pillowcase

Pets should not be allowed where quilts are stored because taking care to properly store your quilts on an unused bed and then allowing dogs and cats to sleep on the quilts defeats the purpose of keeping the quilts free of dust, dirt, and debris, not to mention scratches, rips, tears, chews, and worse.

Quilt courtesy of Helen Squire. Untitled, 73" x 94".

Basic Quilt Care

<u>Cleaning</u>

Before any type of cleaning attempt, make any necessary repairs.

Each quilt presents unique problems and should be examined carefully for the kinds of fabrics it contains, the techniques used to construct it, and its overall condition before any attempt at cleaning is made. When in doubt about at-home cleaning, don't try it. Seek the advice of a professional restorer or conservator if you're convinced a quilt must be cleaned. (See Resources on page 44 for ways to locate these professionals.)

Quilts made from plant materials such as cotton or linen should never be cleaned by a commercial dry cleaner; the chemicals, heat, and large-load tumbling can be very harmful. Quilts made from animal products such as silk and wool can sometimes be dry-cleaned successfully. Quilts made of mixed materials should be discussed with textile professionals.

Quilt, detail. Full quilt on page 13.

Vacuuming

The safest cleaning method is to vacuum the quilt. Dirt, dust, dead insects, or insect eggs all cause damage and can be removed by vacuuming.

Place a screen between the quilt and the vacuum's round dust attachment. Use a low suction setting and slow or up-and-down strokes to prevent harmful pulling.

Bind the edges of abrasive screens with cotton or masking tape to prevent sharp edges from damaging the quilt. If you clean the screen following each use, it can be used repeatedly.

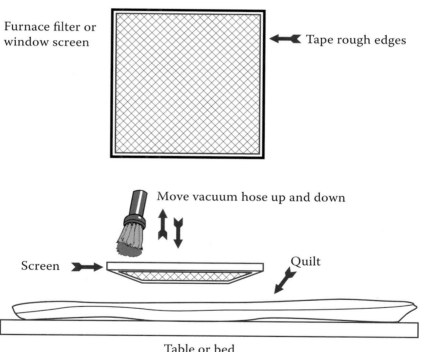

Furnace filter or window screen

Tape rough edges

Move vacuum hose up and down

Screen

Quilt

Table or bed

Although vacuuming will not remove certain types of stains, it may be all that is necessary to adequately clean the quilt.

Basic Quilt Care

Wet Cleaning

The quilt conservator's term for "washing" is "wet cleaning." Wet cleaning should be done only if it won't harm your quilt.

Wet cleaning at home is difficult at best with uncertain results; it is a long, slow, physically demanding process when done as directed. Even if you do everything correctly, you may be unhappy with the results.

Wet quilts are heavy, unwieldy, and the fibers are most prone to damage when wet. In trying to help the quilt by cleaning it, you may be doing it harm.

If you have determined that risking wet cleaning at home is what you want to do, follow the Wet Cleaning steps that follow thoroughly and carefully. Read through the entire process before beginning; timing and logistics are important.

The Wet Cleaning Process

If the water available is hard, use distilled, deionized, filtered, or soft water for wet cleaning or spot wet cleaning. If your water is obtained from a well, well water testing kits are readily available. Hard water contains minerals such as iron that can leave yellowing deposit stains. You can determine the mineral content of publicly provided water by asking about it at your water utility company. You can reduce the chlorine content of water by allowing it to air out for a couple of hours, i.e., fill the tub and walk away. Come back later to wash your quilt.

Soap should not be used because of the scum residue it produces. Pure anionic detergents (sodium lauryl sulfate) such as Orvus˙ are suggested by recognized conservators. Sodium lauryl sulfate has a neutral pH. A half ounce of detergent per gallon of water is recommended. Do not add vinegar or other acids to the rinse water as it will change the neutral pH of the water.

Wet cleaning should be done on a clear, dry day when the quilt may be dried flat outdoors in the shade. Place a clean white cotton mattress pad or cotton blanket on the grass to receive the wet quilt. Lay out the quilt and cover it with a clean white sheet.

Materials to have on hand:
Cotton swabs
Hand-held hairdryer with cool setting
Clean bathtub rinsed free of potentially damaging soaps
    and residues
Non-ionic detergent
Neutral water supply
White mattress pads and/or white towels
Prepared drying surface covered with a clean white sheet
Covering sheet(s)
One or two oscillating fans for drying (optional)

Step 1:

Dye test all fabrics before doing anything else, and if any fabric bleeds, STOP. To dye test:

A. Dampen a cotton swab with room temperature water and press it against the fabric in an inconspicuous place to see if any dye comes off. Do this to each different fabric on the quilt. If any fabric bleeds, STOP. Use a hair dryer on the cool setting to dry the fabric. If none of the fabrics are affected by plain water, proceed to B.

B. Using a non-ionic detergent at the proper concentration (see page 16) on a soft, clean cloth, test each fabric as you did with plain water. If any fabric bleeds, STOP. If none of the fabrics are affected, proceed to Step 2.

Step 2:

Prepare a bath of clear tepid water and detergent in a bathtub to a depth of six to eight inches.

Create a cradle or sling for lowering and raising the quilt from its wet bath to reduce stress, strain, and tearing. The cradle should be made of nylon or fiberglass, such

Basic Quilt Care

as a window screen. Tape over any rough, sharp or protruding edges. Unfold the quilt and drape it in the cradle accordion-style so that water can penetrate it evenly.

Wet cleaning cradle or sling

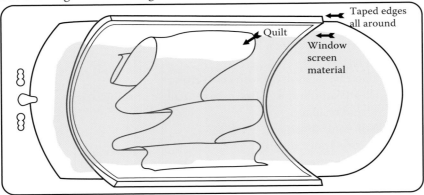

Step 3:

Lower the quilt into the water, gently pressing the water through the accordion folds. Keep the quilt immersed and still; move the water through it, not vice versa. The quilt may benefit from soaking for several hours.

Step 4:

Without removing the quilt, open the bath drain and allow the water to run out. Pull the far side of the cradle gently toward you against the side of the tub to remove water. Do not squeeze or wring the quilt. Soaking in water may be all that is needed to adequately clean a quilt.

Removing water

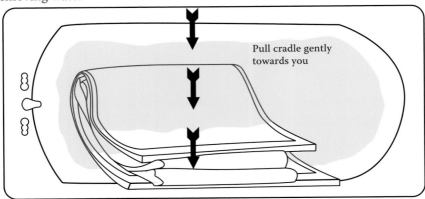

Step 5:

Fill the bath with tepid water again, protecting the quilt from the falling water. If chlorine is an issue, lift the quilt out of the water and set it on a clean surface while the chlorine evaporates.

Step 6:

If necessary, repeat washing (with soap) and rinsing (attending to chlorine issues) until the quilt appears clean. Rinse thoroughly until the water is clear. This may require multiple rinses—as many as six or eight times. Distilled water may be used as a final rinse to remove tap water impurities.

Step 7:

Press the quilt gently to remove excess water. Using the cradle as a support, lift the quilt (it will be heavy) and place it on a clean, white absorbent surface such as a white mattress pad. This is best done by two people. Carefully remove the cradle and loosely roll the quilt in one or more additional white mattress pads or white towels to remove excess water.

Lay the quilt flat on the drying surface right-side down. Gently flip the quilt over every 30 to 45 minutes until it is dry. Remember that the fibers are weakest when wet.

Oscillating fans placed at the four corners of the quilt will hasten the drying process indoors.

If you're drying the quilt outside, place it flat on a flat surface on a clean white sheet. Cover it with another clean white sheet (to protect against sunlight, insects, birds, soil, etc.). Bring the quilt inside and spread it out again to ensure it is completely dry. Do not fold or store the quilt until it is completely dry.

Basic Quilt Care

New Quilts

Many experts recommend treating the components of a new quilt the way the finished quilt will be handled, i.e., prewashing and drying fabrics and washing and drying the quilt when it is finished. Whether you take these steps or not, protect newly made quilts by displaying and storing them as described on pages 6-13, respectively.

Avoid washing quilts when vacuuming, airing, or spot cleaning would suffice.

Restrict activities and exposure to products that would stress the quilt.

Repair an unstitched seam or other minor damage as soon as it happens to prevent further deterioration.

Keep accurate records of your quilts. Label quilts with the date the quilt was made, the name and location of the quiltmaker, the quilt's name, and any other information particular to the quilt.

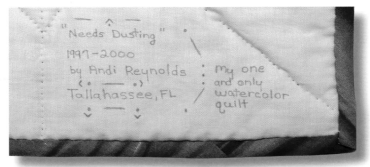

All quilts should be appraised and insured. This may simply involve noting the quilt's appraised value on your homeowner's insurance policy. Check with your insurance agent for policy requirements. See page 27 to locate a certified quilt appraiser. See page 25 for detailed insurance information.

Restoration/Repair

Any restoration or repair made should be reversible. A professional restorer will be familiar with the fabrics that are fragile as a result of the dyes and chemicals used at the time of their manufacture. The choice of materials for repair and restoration should maintain the integrity of the quilt. If deterioration has occurred, how the item is handled and stored can make a huge difference to its longevity.

Questions to ask a professional restorer include:
• What is the age of this quilt and does it have any historical sigificance?
• What is the best approach to prolong the life of this quilt?
• If you work on this quilt, what will you do and how long will it take?
• How much will it cost?
• Are vintage or reproduction fabrics being used for the repair?
• What has been your training?
• How is the cost determined?
• Explain what is intended to be done in the repair.

A professional restorer will submit a complete itemized list of suggested treatments. Each treatment will be accompanied by a cost.

The client will elect what they want (or can afford) to have done. Usually a fee is charged for this service and deducted from the final bill. It is customary that the item is not sent until the work is scheduled.

History and ethics require that a record of repair and/or restoration be kept on each quilt. The information should include when the work was done and by whom, where the work is located on the quilt and the materials used, and the name of the quilt and the owner.

Displaying Quilts

Quilts are visually pleasing and we want to see them, but it is important to balance that pleasure with what is best for the preservation of the quilt.

Location

Keep quilts out of direct or indirect sunlight or strong artificial light; all can cause fading and make fabrics brittle. Filters are available to reduce the damage from fluorescent lights.

Walls that face windows may not seem to receive direct light but they are poor choices for quilt display.

If quilts are displayed on wood surfaces such as quilt racks, protect the quilt from the wood with muslin or acid-free paper. Several coats of polyurethane may also be used to coat the wood.

Quilts should not be displayed where they will be exposed to odors, smoke, soil, insects, other animal damage, harmful moisture, or where they can be easily handled.

Lonestar quilt courtesy of Andi Milam Reynolds. 90" x 90", maker and date unknown.

Shipping Quilts

No matter where you are shipping one or more quilts, each quilt should have identification attached to it, including the owner's name and address.

Place the quilt in a clean cloth bag labeled with your name and address and then into a clear plastic bag also labeled (white or black bags may be mistaken for trash bags). Place the wrapped quilt in a sturdy box. If the quilt fits snugly in the box, place a safety layer of cardboard where any opening knife may cut.

Include a color photo of the quilt in the bag with your name and contact information and why you're sending the quilt: the name of the exhibit it's intended for; the title of your proposal, book, or magazine article; or the contest you're entering.

Enclose a packing list with the box that includes your name and contact information and a list of the quilts in the box. Write the outside label legibly with permanent ink or protect the label with a clear plastic covering. Seal all edges of the box with tape to keep out moisture. Remember that the box will most likely be opened by a sharp knife, so DO NOT PACK THE QUILT TOO TIGHTLY. Consider protecting the quilt with a layer of cardboard or other packing material all around.

DO NOT USE THE WORD "QUILT" ANYWHERE ON THE OUTSIDE OF THE BOX, INCLUDING THE ADDRESS. For example, instead of "American Quilter's Society," write "AQS." Take precautions when using a commercial packing store; do not discuss the value of the items you are shipping with store employees. See page 26 about buying shipping insurance.

Shipping Quilts

Send your quilts early in the week so they do not sit around a warehouse or loading dock over the weekend, or send them overnight so they arrive by Friday.

If you are sending multiple quilts or multiple boxes of quilts, consider packing them either one quilt to a box and sending them on subsequent days, or put two or three quilts in a box and send the several boxes on subsequent days. This prevents having all of your quilts on the one truck that gets into an accident or burns down in a warehouse fire.

If this seems like overkill, it isn't. The condition in which many boxes reach their destination is terrible, no matter who the shipper is; none is better or safer than another. But don't panic; with proper precautions, thousands of quilts are shipped safely every year.

This box arrived torn on one side and ripped open at the end. The quilt inside was not in a plastic bag. Amazingly, it wasn't damaged.

Insuring Quilts

The following information provided by Bradley Butzke & Ryan Butzke, Professional Insurance Agents, Northbrook Ins., Menomonee Falls, Wisconsin.

Quilts are valuable, whether family quilts, antiques you have collected, or quilts you have made. They should be appraised and insured. See page 27 about quilt appraisals. Below are some of the several options available to obtain insurance coverage for your quilts.

Homeowner's Policies

Homeowner's policies are not uniform with regard to protection for your quilts. It is important to know how your homeowner's policy will cover your quilts in the event of a loss. Always consult with your agent to see exactly what your policy covers.

There are several levels of coverage. A standard homeowner's insurance policy is written for actual cash value replacement, which is depreciated by age and use and the policy deductible applies. An endorsed homeowner's insurance policy is written for replacement cost in which the item will be replaced in like, kind and quality. The value the owner has placed on the item can be challenged by the insurance company. The policy deductible also applies. A written appraisal is suggested.

To avoid the deductible and/or depreciation, an inland marine policy to include a fine arts floater may be desirable. It is the broadest endorsement to your homeowner's insurance policy. It provides additional (pre)agreed value insurance coverage without a deductible or depreciation for specific items that are scheduled (listed). This type of coverage requires a written appraisal.

Commercial Lines or Business Insurance

This type of insurance policy covers those things that are directly owned by your business and are used only by the business, such as quilts, sewing samples, longarm quilting machines, office equipment, supplies, etc.

Insuring Quilts

Shipper's Insurance

This is insurance that you can purchase from the shipper of your item for individual instances. Purchasing the shipper's insurance may not be necessary if the destination carries applicable insurance, as AQS does. Check with the venue with regard to the limits of their coverage. Their coverage may or may not cover transportation to and from the venue. It is likely that there will be a maximum amount of coverage without an appraisal that they will offer while the quilt is in their possession. Many will accept a written appraisal as to the value of the quilt and insure it accordingly on their policy.

AQS disclaimer: The best resource for questions and specific explanations is your insurance agent.

Having a quilt appraised for insurance coverage is a primary way to protect the quilt financially in case of loss or damage. Appraisals also provide a basis for selling or donating a quilt. Furthermore, they often provide a record of provenance or construction details that might be lost otherwise.

Lonestar Quilt, detail. Full quilt on page 22.

The Importance of Quilt Appraisals

You can be confident of the services of an AQS-certified appraiser. These appraisers have been successfully tested on knowledge or accuracy of:

- Textile dates
- Construction techniques
- Pattern recognition skills
- Appraised value

In addition, appraisers are required to recertify every three years. Professional Development classes and ongoing educational opportunities are offered to Certified Appraisers through the AQS program. Each appraiser has agreed to a Code of Ethical Practice and to abide by Uniform Standards of Professional Appraisal Practices (USPAP).

All AQS-certified appraisers are qualified to evaluate antique and newly-made traditional and non-traditional quilts. A qualified appraiser will advise a client if a quilt warrants being appraised.

For a list of appraisers certified by AQS or for information regarding appraisal classes, visit our website: www.americanquilter.com (click on "Quilt World Connections") or contact Karen Weaver:
karen@aqsquilt.com or 270-898-7903.

Why an Appraisal Is Necessary

Insurance companies will not accept self-appraisals of quilts. If you are the owner, you cannot determine the insurance value; the insurance company considers you an interested party. Therefore, the value must be determined by a knowledgeable, disinterested party.

Since each quilt is unique, a separate value must be determined for each one.

The Importance of Quilt Appraisals

This must be done by an AQS-certified quilt appraiser. If the insured quilt is lost or damaged, the owner should receive enough money to purchase or remake a similar item of like and kind. The insurance industry refers to the amount of compensation as "actual cash value," since the textile is one of a kind and cannot be duplicated.

An AQS-certified appraiser will determine value based on factual data and other relevant criteria such as a physical examination of the quilt.

Keep your quilt's appraisal stored with your other important legal and financial documents, i.e., in a place such that if the quilt is lost, the appraisal is safe. You may be asked to provide a copy of the appraisal when exhibiting your quilt.

Becoming Certified as a Quilt Appraiser

- The American Quilter's Society provides a number of learning opportunities in appraisal-related lectures and classes during their annual shows. Would-be appraisers can learn what AQS expects in terms of becoming certified.

- Study publications on quilt and fabric dating, quilt pattern recognition, historical trends, and state quilt documentation projects. Perform appraisals; no candidate will be tested or certified without appraisal experience.

- Avail yourself of the ever-updated information on quilts and quilt history from the Alliance for American Quilts, the Quilt Index, and the International Quilt Study Center, as well as museums devoted to quilts or with significant quilt collections.

Attend quilt and gallery shows, museum exhibits, and antique quilt shows.

Talk to dealers who buy and sell quilts in your area.

Ask to observe or assist a certified quilt appraiser.

If you are an appraiser of quilted textiles and wish certification by the American Quilter's Society, request an application form (available at www.americanquilter.com). Complete and return the form by June 1 of any year to be considered for testing the following calendar year. Your paperwork is evaluated by members of the AQS Appraiser Certification Program Committee. Applicants who qualify are scheduled for testing. Panels of certified appraisers conduct written and verbal evaluations of your appraisal skills.

Certifications apply for three years. Recertification is granted with the completion and report of continuing education requirements and appraisal activity.

For more information or to request an application for certification testing, contact the AQS Appraiser Certification Program: Karen Weaver, karen@aqsquilt.com or 270-898-7903.

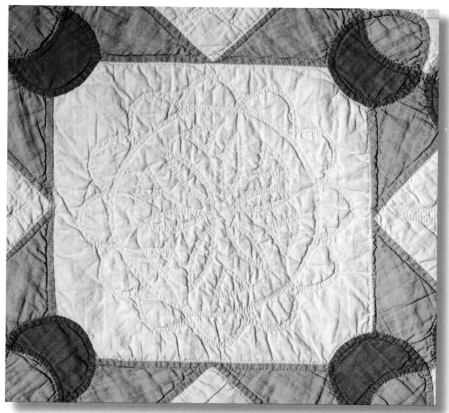

Untitled quilt, detail. Full quilt on page 13.

Glossary of Quilt Terms

Acetate
synthetic fiber made from cellulose acetate; soft and pliable; resembles silk.

Acid-free
inert material used in storage of old or new textiles; may be buffered or non-buffered; appears as tissue paper for use in folds of quilts and as boxes and shelf liners.

Acrylic
synthetic fiber made of a combination of coal, air, water, oil and limestone; soft, lightweight, often used in place of wool.

Aniline and synthetic dyes
dyes in a wide range of colors available after 1856 for weaving and printing textiles. Colors produced by these dyes are bright, inexpensive, and harsh.

Antique
something made long ago, generally 100 years or more.

Appliqué
to put or lay on; the process of sewing small pieces onto a larger background piece.

Appraise
to estimate the value or quality of an item.

Appraiser
a person authorized to fix the value of property; a person who appraises.

Artificial silk
an early name for rayon.

Artistic merit
the value something has by virtue of its art or artistic quality.

Asymmetrical
design which is balanced without mirror imaging.

Bagheera
a velvet with a crease resistant surface and uncut pile.

Batik
one of the oldest methods for dyeing cloth; the application of a liquefied wax, paste, starch, resin, or clay to cloth, which then solidifies, thereby resisting dyes; after dyeing the resist is removed.

Batiste
a fine, lightweight, plain weave cloth, originally linen, silk, or wool but now found in cotton and cotton blends.

Batting

a fibrous material, natural, synthetic or a combination of these used as the middle layer of a quilt; also referred to as fill, filling or wadding.

Bearding

a fiber migration or penetration of batting through top and/or bottom fabrics of a quilt.

Binding

the finished, applied or corded edge of a quilt; self-made or commercially purchased.

Blend

a cloth made of two or more separate fiber contents.

Block printed

the oldest printing method; employs carved wood blocks to apply color to cloth.

Block

a unit, often formed of many parts, which is usually repeated a number of times in the quilt top; typically square or rectangular in shape and usually assembled in rows (strips) horizontally and vertically to form the quilt's design; may be separated by lattice or sashing strips.

Blue resist

fabric patterned in white designs preserved on a blue background; sometimes used for entire quilt tops or backs; chemical, paste or wax is applied to white fabric before it is dyed with woad or indigo.

Border

a width or multiple widths of simple or elaborate construction used to give a frame to the body of the quilt; also used to add length or width.

Boutis

French wholecloth textile consisting of 2 layers with corded designs.

Broadcloth

a smooth, fine-woven cloth of cotton, wool, silk, rayon, or synthetics, various weights wider than 27" cloth.

Brocade

a cloth woven in raised designs with several colors, usually not reversible.

Broderie perse

appliquéd pieces of chintz printed with flowers, foliage, birds, animals and human figures; placed in new combinations of these figures on a cloth foundation.

Glossary of Quilt Terms

Calendar finishes
a variety of finishes produced by running cloth between rollers to apply heat and pressure; types of finishes include glazed, moiré, chased, and water-marked.

Calico
a term originally used to describe cottons with small scale designs imported from Calcutta.

Calimanco
a glossy woolen cloth, checkered or brocaded.

Cambric
a fine, thin white fabric made of linen or cotton that resembles linen.

Carded cotton
cotton fibers that have been carded but not combed. Cards have wire that straighten and clean the fibers for spinning yarn or for filling quilts.

Cashmere
a fine, soft wool under the long hair of the cashmere goat or a fine, soft woolen cloth.

Cellulose
plant cell walls.

Challis
a soft and firm twill weave in cotton, rayon, wool, or blends.

Chambray
a plain weave cloth with a colored warp and a white weft.

Cheater cloth
fabrics preprinted with recognized quilt patterns (designs) as an overall print or blocks.

Check
a fabric made of any fibers in plain weave with colored warp and weft stripes intersecting at right angles to form squares.

Chenille
a thick, firm fabric with a fluffy yarn inserted in a woven or knitted background.

Chintz
a closely woven cotton cloth usually printed in multicolored floral designs, often glazed.

Cigar silks
an advertisement premium often found in boxes of expensive cigars.

Circa
accepted as a time period of about ten years on either side of the given date.

Glossary of Quilt Terms

Collection
a group of related items.

Combed cotton
fibers that have been treated with a process that removes shorter fibers and impurities from carded cotton for fine, tightly woven cloth.

Comforter/comfort
a textile of three layers tied together rather than quilted. [See image on page 22.]

Commemorative
made to preserve the memory of; to call to remembrance a person, place, or event, often depicted on the work.

Conservation
preserving from any further deterioration; protecting from loss or from being used up or wasted.

Contemporary
belonging to or living in the same period; having to do with the present time.

Copper plate printing
employing engraved metal plates to apply color to a cloth; introduced in the second half of the 18th century.

Cording
stitched parallel lines which have been padded.

Corduroy
a pile cloth made of cotton or blend with plain or twill weave; the filling threads usually form vertical ribs; without ribs, ribless corduroy.

Cotton
a natural cellulose fiber; the soft, white fibers in a fluffy mass surrounding the seeds of the plant of the mallow family; widely used in making threads and fabric; also used as batting.

Couching
an embroidery technique in which one element (i.e., wicking) is laid over the cloth and then stitched to it by another, usually finer element (i.e., thread).

Coverlet
a bed covering that may or may not be quilted but has no batting.

Crazy Quilt
style popular late 19th century (Victorian Era); irregular patchwork embellished with embroidery beads, etc.

Crepe
a silk, cotton, rayon, or woolen cloth with a dull, crinkled surface.

Glossary of Quilt Terms

Crepe de chine
any soft, thin, medium weight silk; crepeline.

Cretonne
a thin decorator cotton fabric, often large floral or paisley pattern in twill weave.

Crocking
dye transfer that occurs from wear in dry conditions.

This unwashed vintage Dresden Plate top shows crocking. Photo courtesy of Anita Shackelford, Bucyrus, Ohio, top owner.

Damask
a firm, shiny reversible linen, silk, or cotton fabric woven on a jacquard loom using a blend of plain and stain weave to create complex patterns.

Date
to mark the time at which a thing happens; to find or give the date of a thing.

Dealer
a person who trades; any person engaged in buying and selling.

Denim
strong twilled cotton cloth with dark blue or brown warp and white weft.

Diagonal set
series of blocks joined together at a diagonal angle, on point.

Dimity
a fine cotton cloth, usually woven with additional threads at intervals in striped or cross-barred arrangements.

Direct printing
cloth (usually white) is printed on directly as it passes between rollers; sometimes called application, commercial, roller, or cylindrical printing. Each color requires a separate plate or roller.

Discharge printing
cloth is dyed and then bleached out in certain areas, which are then direct printed with new color; new colorants may be mixed with the bleach to replace the original color. Fabric is uniformly colored on both sides.

Documentation
something written or printed which gives information or proof of some fact; to provide with references as proof of absolute fact.

Echo quilting
a quilt line repeated over the surface at even measure intervals; often used to fill in a background area; the first line is generally parallel to the edges of a pieced or appliquéd shape so that the repeated lines "echo" that shape.

Embossed
any fabric which has a design (in relief) that has been made by pressing the cloth between heated rollers.

Embroidery
the art of working raised designs in cloth with a needle and embroidery thread; thread can be silk, cotton, rayon, etc.

Fabric
any woven, felted or knitted cloth.

Fair market value
the price that property would sell for on the open market. It is the price that would be agreed on between a willing buyer and a willing seller, with neither being required to act, and both having reasonable knowledge of the relevant facts.

Fill (filling)
another term for batting.

Flax
a plant from which cellulose fiber is spun into linen thread and/or made into linen cloth.

Flock
small dots of fibers fixed in the cloth in a pattern or as a series of dots.

Foundation pieced
patches sewn on a textile or paper base.

Gauze
a very thin, loosely woven silk, linen, rayon or cotton cloth; easily seen through.

Gingham
a cotton cloth generally checkered or striped in two or more colors, woven with multiple stranded warps and wefts.

Glossary of Quilt Terms

Glazing
a finish on cotton which gives a shiny finish, often used on chintz. Starch was used early for glazing; newer chemical finishes withstand many washings.

Greige goods
woven, unfinished fabric straight off the loom.

Grosgrain
a finely ribbed fabric; a finish treatment for ribbon.

Hand
the way a textile feels.

HAP
an English term meaning to cover; a flannel-backed, wool-tied comforter commonly found in rural areas of Pennsylvania.

Heat-transfer printing
a printing method for cloth; designs from treated paper are transferred to cloth via heat and pressure.

Hemp
the coarse, tough fiber of the cannabis plant, used for cordage.

Henrietta cloth
a soft, worsted, weft-faced twill fabric of cotton or wool.

Homespun
cloth with a rough, uneven weave; originally made in the home, later reproduced commercially (known as early mill).

Ikat
the process of creating designs on fabric by first wrapping and dyeing the segments of yarn prior to weaving.

Indigo
deep blue-violet dyestuff obtained from various plants; now usually made synthetically.

Insurance value/replacement value
a monetary value assigned to any object (quilt) for use in the event of damage or loss; what it would cost to replace an item with like and kind.

Iridescent
cloth woven with two different colors in the warp and weft causing change in color when the fabric moves.

Jacquard
an extremely complex weave in long pattern repeats on fabric; reversible colors and patterns on the front and back of the fabric.

Jute
a plant fiber used in making rope or sacks.

Kersey
a coarse, cheap, ribbed woolen cloth.

Kits
commercially prepared designs, stamped or numbered with fabric included, ready to be pieced, appliquéd or embroidered. May include precut fabrics and instructions for finishing.

Lamé
a fabric either knitted or woven with a metallic yarn in the warp, filling, or both.

Lattice
a grid of lines; horizontals, verticals, or diagonals with open spaces in between; in quiltmaking these lines (strips) are used as separators or frames.

Lawn
a sheer, crisp linen or cotton cloth with a plain weave.

Linen
a fabric made from flax fibers; strong, lustrous, and very absorbent; in various weights and in plain or damask weaves.

Linsey-woolsey
a strong, coarse fabric made of linen and wool or cotton and wool.

Loom
device used to weave yarn into fabric.

Madder
a plant from which red dye is obtained.

Madras
a soft cotton woven with plaid, checked or striped pattern; dyed with vegetable dyes which bleed when laundered.

Mercerized
treatment for cotton thread or fabrics; an alkali solution is used to strengthen it, give it a gloss and give it affinity to dye.

Merino
the finest woolen cloth from merino sheep.

Mildew
a whitish coating or a discoloration on cotton, linen, leather, etc., produced by a parasitic fungi.

Mitered
a 45-degree angle joining; typically used at a corner; often used on borders and bindings.

Glossary of Quilt Terms

Moiré
a rippled watermark pattern found in silks, taffetas or acetates; created by printing or calendaring.

Mola
a decorative textile object made of cotton cloth, incorporating appliqué, reverse appliqué, and sometimes embroidery; usually pictorial; developed by the Cuna people of the San Blas Islands; not to be confused with Pa Ndau.

Muslin
a fine, thin cotton cloth; can be made of blends.

Nap
a soft or fuzzy surface texture.

Nylon
synthetic fabric from chemicals derived from coal, water, air, petroleum, agricultural byproducts and natural gas; are not weakened by mildew and absorb little water.

Organdy
a stiff, lightweight fabric, usually cotton.

Orleans
plain weave warp is thin cotton or silk and weft is worsted wool.

Outing flannel
a soft cotton cloth napped on both sides; a twill or plain weave.

Overdyeing
to dye cloth with a second color over another.

Overprint
a print applied on top of a piece of cloth which has already been printed.

Paisley
a soft woolen cloth with elaborate and colorful patterns; originally woven to imitate elaborate Kashmir shawls; scrolled designs woven and printed today.

Palampore
a one-piece, mordant-painted and resist-dyed bed covering imported from India; those imported in the 18th century often featured scenes abundant with plant life, animals, birds, etc.; sometimes made into quilts with border strips attached.

Patchwork
section of cloth sewn together in a planned or random design to make a larger piece of goods.

Pa Ndau

an appliqué technique typical of the Hmong people of Southeast Asia; reverse appliqué designs that are usually geometric and often highly symmetrical; not to be confused with molas.

Percale – a closely woven (200 threads per inch) cotton cloth with a smooth finish.

PFD (prepared for dyeing fabric)

unbleached cotton that has no optic whiteners added.

Photo transfer

the practice of printing photographs onto fabric to use in quilts.

Pieced

separate fabric shapes sewn to each other to create an overall pattern or design.

Pills

small fiber balls which appear on the surface of cloth; usually found on wools or synthetics.

Pima cotton

a fine, extra-long-staple cotton; used in quality cotton goods.

Plaid

pattern of interesting stripes in both warp and weft; silk, cotton or wool may be plain weave or twill.

Plain weave

the simplest weave, which has one filling passing over and under each warp thread; tabby weave.

Polished cotton

a plain weave cloth with a permanent glaze; less sheen than chintz.

Polyester

a synthetic fiber; used independently or with other fibers to make a blend.

Pongee

woven silk cloth with uneven threads of raw silk.

Preserve

to keep from harm or change.

Professional

an individual trained in some activity to make a living.

Provenance

a source or origin; oral or written.

Quilt

a textile of three layers consisting of top, filler or batting (can be cotton, wool, polyester, blends or old quilts), and a backing, stitched together by hand or machine.

Glossary of Quilt Terms

Quilting
stitching together, in a decorative or utilitarian design, the three layers of a quilt.

Ramie
a natural cellulose fiber yielding strong, lustrous fiber; similar to flax; often used with other fibers.

Rayon
a fiber made from regenerated cellulose; soft but weak when wet; the first man-made fiber.

Redwork
outline embroidery worked in red cotton floss.

Repair
replacing a part or mending torn or broken areas in a dignified, respectful and reversible state with materials that closely resemble the original materials, which may or may not be available.

Research
a careful hunting for facts or truth about a subject, an inquiry, or investigation.

Resist
a printing method in which a substance that resists dye is applied prior to dyeing; dye does not permeate a resist area, which leaves behind undyed fabric designs; resists may be wax, paste, or chemicals.

Restore
to bring back to the original condition.

Retail
to sell directly to a customer.

Roller printing
a printing technique that enabled a number of colors to be printed almost simultaneously with accurate registration.

Sashiko – a Japanese technique of quilt-type stitching; usually executed with embroidery thread.

Sateen – a firmly woven cotton cloth made to imitate satin.

Satin
a firmly woven silk, rayon, acetate, nylon, or polyester cloth with a very smooth, glossy surface.

Sashing
see lattice.

Screen printing
a method of printing designs using a silk

or nylon gauze; all designs are covered with a non-porous substance; dye is then forced through the uncoated areas to print the fabric placed below; each color applied needs a separate screen.

Seersucker
woven cloth with uneven tension forming stripes and a puckered surface.

Seminole patchwork
patchwork technique using many small bits of cloth developed by Seminole people of Florida; strips of fabric are sewn together, cut into parts and then resewn to create geometric designs.

Sentimental value
a feeling or emotion attached to a possession; cannot be given a monetary value.

Serge
a smooth twill weave wool cloth; durable; develops a hard shine with wear.

Set
an arrangement of blocks or pieces.

Silk
a fiber made by the larvae of certain moths; the only natural filament fiber; made into a fine lustrous cloth in a variety of weaves and weights.

Sleeve
an elongated tube of fabric sewn to the top back of a quilt; used as a rod holder for hanging.

Slub
in silk, a small thick section of fiber; natural occurrences that give a raised and rough texture to the surface; in man-made cloth, artificially created.

Stain
to spoil by discoloring or soiling.

Stencil
to mark or paint with a cutout design sheet; when ink or paint is applied, letters, designs, etc., appear on the surface in the space left open.

Stipple
to cover the surface with close quilting stitches that do not overlap or cross to give a dimpled effect.

Stitching in the ditch
a line of stitching on a quilt hidden in the seam area.

Stitches per inch
the number of quilted stitches in an inch on the top of a quilt.

Glossary of Quilt Terms

Straight set
any blocks placed side by side horizontally and vertically; may be touching or separated by sashing.

Stripe
a long, narrow band of a different color from its surroundings.

Stuffed work
an outline quilted design that has been padded with cotton, yarn or other material to produce a high relief; see trapunto.

Swatch
a cloth sample, small size, which shows pattern and color.

Symmetrical
the correspondence of parts with respect to size, shape and position.

Synthetic
man-made fibers created in a laboratory.

Taffeta
a plain woven glossy silk, acetate, rayon or other synthetic; has characteristic rustle.

Template
a flat piece of material used as a pattern for reproducing a shape.

Textile
a woven fabric; commonly interchanged term with fabric and cloth.

Tradition
the handing down of customs, beliefs, stories, patterns, etc.

Tow
the coarse, broken fibers of flax, hemp or jute; sometimes used as fill.

Trapunto
an Italian word describing an outline quilted design that has been padded with cotton, yarn or other material to produce a high relief; see stuffed work.

Turkey red
madder-dyed cotton; initially done by a secret dyeing process of the Near East producing a distinctive red color; deciphered and replicated by the French in 1765.

Twill
a foundation system of weaving cloth that produces the characteristic diagonal ribs or lines of diamond, herringbone or birds' eye patterns; stronger than plain weave.

Tying

knots are used instead of or in conjunction with quilting on a three-layer textile to hold all layers in place and together.

Velvet

cloth with a thick, short, soft pile on one side; made of silk, rayon, or nylon; the warp is pulled over a needle, making loops which are cut (cut velvet) or uncut (pile velvet).

Velveteen

cotton fabric with a short, close pile; like velvet.

Vintage

old; neither contemporary nor antique; less than 100 years of age.

Visual impact

the ability of a quilt to evoke a response from the viewer.

Warp

yarns placed on the loom to run the length of the cloth, parallel to the edge.

Weft – the cross threads in a woven fabric; also called filling.

Wet cleaning

the washing of a textile to remove soil, stains and discolorations.

White work

white fabrics and threads used to create a surface design; candlewicking, tufting and quilting can be included in this type of needlework.

Woad

a blue dye made from a plant in the cabbage family.

Worsted

cloth made from long, highly twisted smooth fibers; crisp hand with a clear finish.

Woven

the oldest method of turning fiber into yarn into fabric. A loom is set up with the lengthwise (warp) yarns; a shuttle (device to carry yarn) moves across the loom, interlacing the crosswise (weft or filling) yarns in the warp. The weft pattern may be plain, satin or twill.

Resources

Conservation Supplies

Conservation supplies and quilt-related professional services can be accessed through the Internet. Two reputable firms for supplies are Gaylord and Light Impressions. Qualified conservators can be found at www.conservationus.org

Quilt-related Publications Reference List

Included in this reference list are publications that may be helpful to you in your study of quilts. They cover many facets of research that have been done on quilts. However, this is by no means a complete list. Most are readily available from libraries. There are many other good reference materials currently available and new resources are continuing to be published.

Adamson, Jeremy. **Calico & Chintz, Antique Quilts from the Collection of Patricia S. Smith.** Smithsonian Institution, Washington, D.C., 1997. ISBN 1-937311-34-0 (cloth), ISBN 1-937311-35-9 (paper) (also found as ISBN 0937311359)

Allen, Gloria Seaman, and Nancy Gibson Tuckhorn. **A Maryland Album: Quiltmaking Traditions** 1634-1934. Rutledge Hill Press, Nashville, TN, 1995. ISBN 1-55853-341-9 (also found publisher as Thomas Nelson)

Aug, Bobbie A., Sharon Newman, and Paul Kopp. **Calico Man: The Manny Kopp Fabric Collection.** American Quilter's Society, Paducah, KY, 2005. ISBN 1-57432-894-8

Aug, Bobbie A., Sharon Newman, Gerald Roy. **Vintage Quilts: Identifying, Collecting, Dating, Preserving & Valuing.** Collector Books, a division of Schroeder Publishing Co., Inc., Paducah, KY, 2002. ISBN 1-57432-285-0

Aug, Bobbie A., and Gerald Roy. **Antique Quilts & Textiles: A Price Guide to Functional and Fashionable Cloth Comforts.** Collector Books, a division of Schroeder Publishing Co., Inc., Paducah, KY, 2004. ISBN 1574323740 and 978-574323740

Beardsley, John, et. al. **The Quilts of Gee's Bend.** Tinwood Books, Atlanta, GA, 2002. ISBN 0-9653766-4-8

Benberry, Cuesta Ray. **Always There: The African-American Presence in American Quilts.** The Kentucky Quilt Project, Inc., Louisville, KY, 1992. ISBN 880584026 and 978-1880584026

Berenson, Kathryn. **Quilts of Provence: The Art and Craft of French Quiltmaking.** Henry Holt & Co., New York, NY, 1996. ISBN 0-8050-4639-9. (also found publisher as Potter Craft and the date as 2007; ISBN 0307345521 or 978-0307345523)

Bishop, Robert. **The Romance of Double Wedding Ring Quilts.** E. P. Dutton, New York, NY, 1989. ISBN 0-525-48477-9

Brackman, Barbara. **America's Printed Fabrics, 1770-1840.** C&T Publishing, Lafayette, CA, 2004. ISBN 1-57120-255-2

Brackman, Barbara. **Clues in the Calico: A Guide to Identifying and Dating Antique Quilts.** EPM Publications, McLean VA, 1989. ISBN 0-939009-27-7 (also found publisher as Howell Press, Inc.)

Brackman, Barbara. **Encyclopedia of Appliqué: An Illustrated, Numerical Index to Traditional and Modern Patterns.** EPM Publications, Inc., McLean, VA, 1993, 2009. ISBN 0-939009-75-7 (new title is: **Encyclopedia of Appliqué** and ISBN 978-1-57120-651-0)

Brackman, Barbara. **Encyclopedia of Pieced Quilt Patterns.** American Quilter's Society, Paducah, KY, 1993. ISBN 0-089145-815-8

Brackman, Barbara. **Making History: Quilts and Fabrics from 1890-1970.** C&T Publishing, Lafayette, CA, 2008. ISBN 978-1-57120-453-0

Cochran, Rachel, et al. **New Jersey Quilts 1777 to 1950: Contributions to an American Tradition.** American Quilter's Society, Paducah, KY, 1992. ISBN 0-89145-996-0

Cognac, Camille Dalphond. **Quilt Restoration: A Practical Guide.** EPM Publications, McLean, VA, 1994. ISBN 978-0939009831

Crews, Dr. Patricia Cox, ed. **A Flowering of Quilts.** University of Nebraska Press, Lincoln, NE, 2001. ISBN 0-8032-1513-4

Ducey, Carolyn. **Chintz Appliqué: From Imitation to Icon.** University of Nebraska Press, Lincoln, NE, 2008. ISBN 978-0-9814582-2-9

Eaton, Linda. **Quilts in a Material World: Selections from the Winterthur Museum.** Harry N. Abrams, Inc., New York, NY, 2007. ISBN 0-8109-3012-9

Fox, Sandi. **For Purpose and Pleasure: Quilting Together in Nineteenth-Century America.** Rutledge Hill Press, Nashville, TN, 1995. ISBN 1-55853-337-0 (also found publisher as Thomas Nelson)

Fox, Sandi. **Small Endearments: Nineteenth-Century Quilts for Children and Dolls.** Rutledge Hill Press, Nashville, TN, 1985, 1994. ISBN 1-55853-312-5

Resources

Frost, Helen Young, and Pam Knight Stevenson. **Grand Endeavors: Vintage Arizona Quilts and Their Makers.** Northland Publishing Co., Flagstaff, AZ, 1992. ISBN 0-87358-547-X

Garoutte Sally, Virginia Gunn, Kathlyn Sullivan, Laurel Horton, eds. **Uncoverings, American Quilt Study Group, San Francisco, CA 1980-present.**

Goldsborough, Jennifer Faulds. **Lavish Legacies.** Maryland Historical Society, Baltimore, MD, 1994, 2005. ISBN 978-0938420392

Granick, Eve Wheatcroft. **The Amish Quilt.** Good Books, Intercourse, PA, 1989, 1994. ISBN 0-934672-74-1 (also found as ISBN 1561481092 and 978-1561481095)

Hanson, Marin F., and Patricia Cox Crews, eds. **American Quilts in the Modern Age,1870-1940.** University of Nebraska Press, Lincoln, NE, 2009. ISBN 978-0-8032-2054-6

Hedges, Elaine, Pat Ferrero, and Julie Silber. **Hearts and Hands, Women, Quilts and American Society.** Rutledge Hill Press, Nashville, TN, 1987. ISBN 1-55853-434-2 (also found as **Hearts and Hands: The Influence of Women & Quilts on American Society;** publisher Quilt Digest Press; ISBN 978-0913327142)

Hefford, Wendy. **The Victoria & Albert Museum's Textile Collection; Design for Printed Textiles in England from 1750-1850.** V&A Publications, London, England, 1992,1999, 2002. ISBN 1-85177-115-8

Herr, Patricia T. **Amish Quilts of Lancaster County.** Schiffer Books (Publishing), Atglen, PA, 2004. ISBN 0-7643-2017-3

Horton, Laurel, ed. **Quiltmaking in America: Beyond the Myths.** Rutledge Hill Press, Nashville, TN, 1994. ISBN 1558533192 (also found Thomas Nelson as publisher)

Kirakofe, Roderick. **The American Quilt: A History of Cloth and Comfort 1750-1950.** Clarkson Potter Publishers, New York, NY, 1993, 2004. ISBN 0-517-57535-3 (1400080967 and 978-1400080960)

Lasansky, Jeannette, ed. **Bits and Pieces: Textile Traditions.** Oral Traditions Project of the Union County Historical Society, Lewisburg, PA, 1991. ISBN 0-81221362-9

Lasansky, Jeannette. **In the Heart of Pennsylvania: 19th and 20th**

Century QuiltmakingTraditions. Oral Traditions Project of the Union County Historical Society, Lewisburg, PA, 1985. ISBN 0-917127-00-5

Lasansky, Jeannette, ed. **On the Cutting Edge: Textile Collectors, Collections and Traditions.** Oral Traditions Project of the Union County Historical Society, Lewisburg, PA, 1994. ISBN 0-917217-08-0

Lasansky, Jeannette, ed. **Pieced by Mother: Over 100 years of Quiltmaking Traditions.** Oral Traditions Project of the Union County Historical Society, Lewisburg, PA, 1987. ISBN 0-917127-02-1

Lasansky, Jeannette, ed. **Pieced by Mother: Symposium Papers.** Oral Traditions Project of the Union County Historical Society, Lewisburg, PA, 1988. ISBN 0-917127-03-X

Meller, Susan, and Joost Elffers. **Textile Designs: Two Hundred Years of European and American Patterns Organized by Motif, Style, Color, Layout, and Period.** Harry N. Abrams, Inc., New York, NY, 1991, 2002. ISBN 0-8109-3853-7 (also found 0810925087)

Montgomery, Florence M. **Textiles in America (1650-1870).** W. W. Norton & Co., New York, NY, 2007. ISBN 978-0-393-73224-5

Nylander, Jane C., & Richard C. Nylander. **Fabrics and Wallpapers for Historic Buildings.** Wiley, Hoboken, NJ, 2005. ISBN 0 0471706558

Orlofsky, Patsy and Myron Orlofsky. **Quilts in America.** Abbeville Press, New York, NY, 1974, 1992. ISBN 1-55859-334-9

Parry, Linda. **The Victoria & Albert Museum's Textiles Collection: British Textiles from 1850-1900.** V&A Publications, London, England, 1993, 1999. ISBN 1-85177-127-1

Perry, Rosalind Webster and Marty Frolli. **A Joy Forever: Marie Webster's Quilt Patterns.** Practical Patchwork, Santa Barbara, CA, 1992. ISBN 0-9620811-7-5

Perry, Rosalind Webster and Marty Frolli. **Marie Webster's Garden of Quilts.** Practical Patchwork, Santa Barbara, CA, 2001. ISBN 0-9620811-8-3

Pettit, Florence Harvey. **America's Printed and Painted Fabrics 1600-1900: All the Ways There Are to Print Upon Textiles.** Hastings House, Winter Park, FL, 1970. ISBN10-1856690067 (also found 0803803400; 978-0803803404)

Pilgrim, Paul D. and Gerald E. Roy. **Victorian Quilts 1875-1900: They Aren't All Crazy.** American Quilter's Society, Paducah, KY, 1995. ISBN 0-89145-846-8

Resources

Prichard, Sue, ed. **Quilts 1700-2010: Hidden Histories, Untold Stories.** V&A Publishing, London, England, 2010. ISBN 9-781851-775958

Rae, Janet, et al. **Quilt Treasures of Great Britain: The Heritage Search of the Quilters' Guild.** Rutledge Hill Press, Nashville, TN, 1995, 1996. ISBN 1-55853-384-2

Safford, Carleton L. and Robert Bishop. **America's Quilts and Coverlets.** E.P. Dutton &Co., Inc., New York, NY, 1972. ISBN 0-525-05395-6 (Of historic value as being the first to delve deeply into the history of quilts.) (also found Random House Value Publishing, 1987; ISBN 10-0517143917)

Sandberg, Gösta. **Indigo Textiles: Technique and History.** Lark Books, Asheville, NC, 1989. ISBN 0-937274-40-2 (also found publisher as Sterling)

Sandberg, Gösta. **The Red Dyes, Cochineal, Madder and Murex Purple: A World Tour of Textile Techniques.** Lark Books, Asheville, NC, 1994. ISBN 1-887874-17-5 (also found publisher as Sterling, 1996)

Schoeser, Mary and Kathleen Dejardin. **French Textiles: From 1760 to the Present.** Trafalgar Square, Chicago, IL, 1992. ISBN 1856690067

Shaw, Robert. **American Quilts: The Democratic Art 1780-2007.** Sterling Publishing Co., New York, NY, 2009. ISBN 978-1-4027-4773-1

Trestain, Eileen Jahnke. **Dating Fabrics: A Color Guide 1800-1960.** American Quilter's Society, Paducah, KY, 1998. ISBN 0-89145-884-0

Trestain, Eileen Jahnke. **Dating Fabrics: A Color Guide 1950-2000.** American Quilter's Society, Paducah, KY, 2005. ISBN 1-57432-883-2

Waldvogel, Merikay. **Patchwork Souvenirs of the 1933 World's Fair.** Rutledge Hill Press, Nashville, TN, 1993. ISBN 1-55853-257-9 (also found Thomas Nelson as publisher)

Waldvogel, Merikay. **Soft Covers for Hard Times: Quiltmaking & The Great Depression.** Rutledge Hill Press, Nashville, TN, 1990. ISBN 1-55853-062-2

Welters, Linda and Margaret T. Ordonez, eds. **Down by the Old Mill Stream: Quilts in Rhode Island.** Kent State University Press, Kent, OH, 2000. ISBN 0-87338-627-2